Contents

For my daughter Samantha
and her help in obtaining
photographs and postcards in Germany
when living in Munich.

Images of War

The German 1918 Offensives in France & Flanders

PHOTOGRAPHS OF THE GERMAN OFFENSIVES IN 1918

John Sheen

Pen & Sword
MILITARY

First published in Great Britain in 2007 by
PEN & SWORD MILITARY
an imprint of
Pen & Sword Books Ltd,
47 Church Street, Barnsley,
South Yorkshire.
S70 2AS

A CIP record for this book is available from the British
Library

ISBN 978 1 84415 6 368

A CIP catalogue record for this book is available from the
British Library.

Printed and bound by CPI UK

Pen & Sword Books Ltd incorporates the Imprints of
Pen & Sword Aviation, Pen & Sword Maritime,
Pen & Sword Military, Wharncliffe Local History, Pen & Sword
Select, Pen & Sword Military Classics and Leo Cooper.
For a complete list of Pen & Sword titles please contact
Pen & Sword Books Limited
47 Church Street, Barnsley, South Yorkshire, S70 2AS, England
E-mail: enquiries@pen-and-sword.co.uk
Website: www.pen-and-sword.co.uk

Introduction

The Germans

On 11 November 1917, General Ludendorff summoned the Chiefs of Staff of the Group of Armies commanded by Crown Prince Rupprecht of Bavaria and the German Crown Prince Wilhelm, to a conference in Mons to discuss plans for 1918. The collapse of the Russian Army allowed the Germans to move around forty divisions from the Eastern Front to the Western Front, thus giving them a numerical superiority, which would allow them to strike a decisive blow in the west and possibly win the war. A number of proposals were put forward at this first conference, but they did not make any final decisions and the staff officers separated to study the problems of any offensives in the west.

By 15 December it was clear that Russia was out of the war and that the number of divisions available could be increased, along with a certain amount of heavy artillery. Troops were given three weeks' training in offensive operations and the best divisions were taken out of the line and put through an intensive training course. Men over the age of thirty-five were sent to the divisions left in the east and men under that age were brought from those divisions to replace the older men. Ammunition and shells were stockpiled and plans prepared. Another conference was held on 27 December 1917 where a number of operations were proposed: 'George', an offensive near Armentieres, possibly combined with 'George II', an offensive near Ypres, 'Mars', an offensive in the Arras area and 'Michael', an offensive on both sides of St Quentin. Other attacks planned included: 'Archangel', an attack by Seventh Army south of the Oise; 'Hector' and 'Achilles', east of Reims; and 'Roland' on the old Champagne battlefield, along with 'Castor' and 'Pollux', two attacks on either side of Verdun.

Preliminary orders were issued on 24 January 1918 and again on 8 February. It was decided that the 'George' offensives were too dependent on the weather; if there was a wet spring the Valley of the Lys would be difficult to cross until possibly May. With the British in possession of Vimy Ridge, the 'Mars' attack was regarded as difficult. 'Hector', 'Achilles' and 'Roland' were kept on hold, whilst 'Castor' and 'Pollux' were abandoned. The main attack would be 'Michael' which was divided into three sub-attacks, 'Michael 1' to be carried out by the left wing of Seventeenth Army, in the direction of Bapaume. 'Michael 2' was the responsibility of Second Army, advancing in the direction of Peronne and 'Michael 3' required the Eighteenth Army to attack towards Ham. Whilst on the French front, diversions and demonstrations would delay the French from sending support to the British.

After several days the right wing of Seventeenth Army would start the 'Mars' offensive, when the artillery had been regrouped and moved to the new sector. Whilst the German High Command was making these plans the British helped them by taking over and extending the British right southwards to the Oise.

The British and French

During the previous two years the British Army had concentrated on attacking the Germans and their positions were almost all of a temporary nature. There was little in the way of solid, well-sited defences with machine gun emplacements and deeply buried signal wires. Furthermore there was a manpower shortage and British divisions had been reduced from twelve to nine fighting battalions, whilst the divisional pioneer battalion had lost one of its companies. The surplus of men created was used to bring the other battalions back up to strength. The British Army in France was used to hard fighting, but the soldiers who had carried out the fighting retreats and defensive battles of 1914 and 1915 had mostly been killed or evacuated as sick and wounded.

The army needed a lot of training in defence and the preparation of defensive positions. In particular the musketry of the infantry left a lot to be desired and the vast majority of men were below a reasonable standard. The British and French knew a German attack was coming; the question was where, and also could they hold on until the Americans arrived in strength? During February 1918 three divisions, 18th (Eastern), 20th (Light) and 66th (2nd East Lancashire), were moved from Fourth Army in Flanders to Fifth Army and in early March 50th (Northumbrian) Division moved south also. A number of artillery units were also sent to Fifth Army, two Army Brigades RFA, ten Heavy Brigades RGA and nine un-brigaded siege batteries along with an Anti-Aircraft Battery.

Sir Douglas Haig designed his plans so as to be able to meet an attack in Flanders and also to meet and deal with an enemy offensive further south on the front of the Third and Fifth Armies. When British Intelligence identified the fact that the German, General von Hutier and his Chief of Staff, General von Sauberzweig, were commanding the German Army opposite Fifth Army, it seemed that the blow would fall on Fifth Army.

Chapter One

Preparation for Attack

Given the success of the British tanks at Cambrai the previous November, the German commanders were keen to have tanks and employ them in the coming offensive. A number of units were formed to recover undamaged and lightly damaged tanks and take them to the rear, where workshop units could repair them and put them back into service against their former owners. Other units were sent out to cannibalise more severely damaged vehicles and to bring back spare parts for the workshops.

At the German Army Headquarters, OHL, orders were issued that, in order to keep the enemy guessing as to where the attack would take place, each army should give the impression that they were about to attack. This was to be done all along the front from Alsace to the sea; in every area rumours, false reports, and movement of civilians away from certain areas took place. On the British front in Flanders, the Sixth and Fourth Armies made demonstrations of increased activity. An extra Army Headquarters appeared in Lorraine, in Champagne from 1 March the preparations for an offensive were made obvious to any observers, whilst on the front commanded by Crown Prince Rupprecht, the preparations for 'George' were very obvious.

The concentration of the vast forces needed for the operation was a massive problem, but the planners solved the problem with complete success. By 15 March all the ammunition was in camouflaged dumps in the forward area. Between 11 and 19 March the extra guns and trench mortars were moved up and were all in position by 20 March. Meanwhile the 60 Infantry Divisions began moving on 16 March; on the night 18/19 March they rested and then moved forward into the forward positions on the following night, thereby letting the assaulting troops prepare and then rest on the night of 20 March.

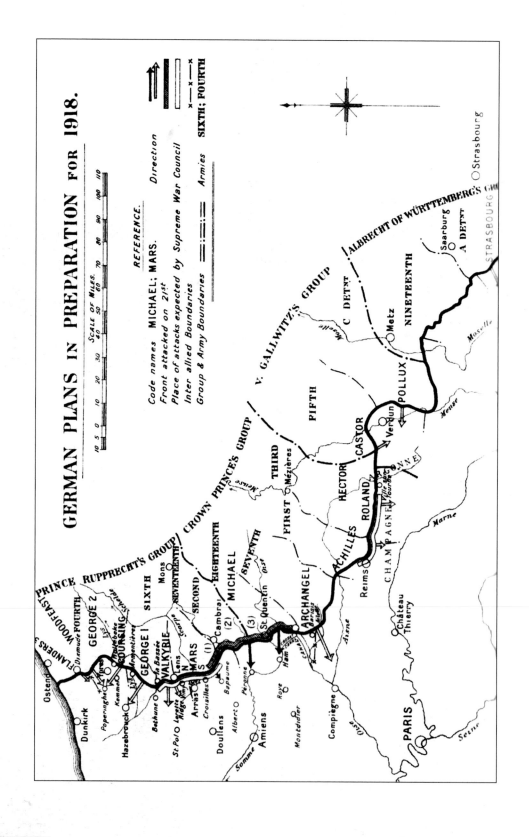

GERMAN PLANS IN PREPARATION FOR 1918.

REFERENCE.

Code names MICHAEL; MARS.   Direction

Front attacked on 21st

Place of attacks expected by Supreme War Council

Inter allied Boundaries

Group & Army Boundaries   Armies   SIXTH; FOURTH

SCALE OF MILES.
10 5 0 10 20 30 40 50 60 70 80 90 100 110

PRINCE RUPPRECHT'S GROUP   CROWN PRINCE'S GROUP   V. GALLWITZ'S GROUP   ALBRECHT OF WÜRTTEMBERG'S GR.

WOODEEAST
FLANDERS 3
FLANDERS FOURTH
GEORGE 2
COURSING
GEORGE 1
SIXTH
SEVENTEENTH
VALKYRIE
SECOND
MARS
EIGHTEENTH
MICHAEL
SEVENTH
FIRST
THIRD
FIFTH
HECTOR
ACHILLES
ROLAND
CASTOR
POLLUX
NINETEENTH
C DET.NT
A DET.NT
STRASBOURG

Ostend
Dunkirk
Poperinghe
Kemmel
Hazebrouck
Bethune
La Bassée
Lens
St Pol
Legise
Ridge
Arras
Croisilles
Doullens
Albert
Bapaume
Péronne
Roye
Amiens
Montdidier
Compiègne
Mons
Cambray
(1)
(2)
(3)
St. Quentin
Ham
ARCHANGEL
Reims
Château Thierry
PARIS
Méziéres
Verdun
Metz
Saarburg
Strasbourg

Somme
Oise
Aisne
Marne
Seine
Meuse
Moselle
Mosette
CHAMPAGNE
Fourth
Ville sur

Members of a recovery crew from Fuhrpark Kolon 787 inspect C51 for possible spares.

Posted at Field Post Office Number 72, by a soldier named Hauptvogel serving with Fuhrpark Kolon Number 787, this view of C51 is quite early with German soldiers examining the wreckage. Note the camouflage net is still hanging over the side of the tank. Compare this to the later photograph of the same tank in Chapter 7.

C47, knocked out in Fontaine, soon to be recovered by the Germans.

German infantry passing C47, which now has a winch rope attached and will soon be on its way to a workshop to be repaired or cannibalised.

The German workshops at Charleroi. Female Tank C14 is being repaired by a crew of German mechanics. Between the two men on the rear of the tank is the inscription GEBORGEN DURCH, K FLAK 2, Bei Cambrai 15.12.17. SECURED THROUGH, Anti Aircraft Battery No 2, At Cambrai, 15.12.17.

A German soldier named 'Willi' poses beside a knocked-out tank. Judging by the postmark on the card he was a member of an unknown Fuhrpark Kolon, probably employed salvaging spares.

A female tank in St Quentin; having been repaired it now has German 'Iron Cross' markings. By 21 March the Germans had five tanks ready to go back into action.

Infantry are brought up to the rear area by motor lorry convoy.

The crew of a 58cm railway gun prepare it for firing.

The crew of a 38cm railway gun remove the camouflage netting in order to get the gun ready for its deadly work.

An NCO and a comparatively small gunner prepare the ammunition for the gun whilst the rest of the crew are around the gun.

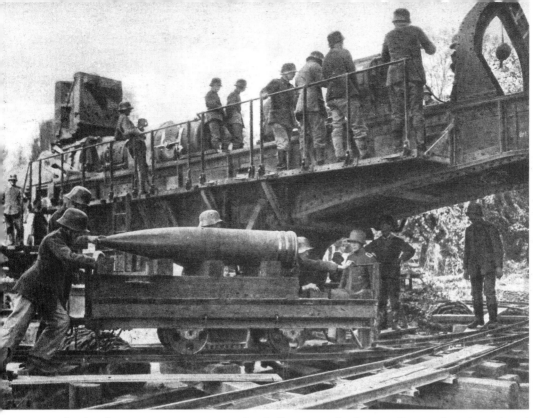

It takes four gunners to transport the shell, on a small railway trolley, to where it can be winched up onto the gun.

The shell is now behind the breech and some of the crew begin to push it home; on the left a ram rod lies waiting to be used in the final push.

The crew stand clear and another shell hurtles towards the British rear area, possibly to land on the headquarters or railway installations around St Pol or Doullens.

A 42cm mortar. Manufactured by Krupps, this weapon could fire a 900kg shell over 10 km.

A heavy mortar is moved into position prior to the beginning of the barrage that will begin the battle.

Another railway gun weighing in at 140 tonnes, this time on the French Front and able to fire at Laon (128 kms), Beaumont (109 kms) and Chateau Thierry (87 kms).

Men of the 49th Infantry Regiment behind the line prior to the battle. Part of the 4th Division, they attacked on the front between Doignies and Hermies near Bapaume on 21 March 1918. The regiment had its depot at Gnesen in Pommerania.

Members of a mobile signals unit pose for the camera; one man can be seen sitting in the cab of the lorry which is hidden from view by the amount of men standing on and around it.

The telephone exchange of a field artillery regiment.

Telephonunterstand an der Westfront.

Chapter Two

21 March 1918
'Michael' – the Kaiser's Battle

At around 1700 hours on 20 March 1918 a ground mist began to rise all along the front held by Third and Fifth Armies; it rose steadily until by 2100 hours it was a fog which got thicker as the night went on and when patrols went out they discovered that No Man's Land was empty, but at many gaps had been cut in the German barbed wire. When the patrols neared these gaps they encountered strong resistance. Owing to the weather along the British Front they only carried out a few raids and these were generally unsuccessful. The prisoners that were taken were very keen to be sent to the rear as quickly as possible, which confirmed to the British that an attack was imminent. Indeed one prisoner definitely told an officer who questioned him in German that the attack would start at 0900 hours. Given this information some British divisions 'Stood To' and began manning their battle stations. From 0330 hours the British Artillery began firing on suspected German forming-up positions and counter-battery work. On 61st (2nd South Midland) Division front at St Quentin, the front was covered in gas, released from canisters especially located for such an eventuality.

At 0440 hours on 21 March 1918, a tremendous bombardment opened along the front of Fifth Army and most of Third Army. Heavy and light trench mortars concentrated on the British front trenches, whilst all forms of artillery, field guns, howitzers and heavy siege artillery concentrated on vital targets. The staff and observers did their work well and with great accuracy the fire fell on headquarters, telephone exchanges, railway installations and battery positions. Telephone lines which had been deeply buried were cut and communication between division and brigade and the forward units practically ceased. Many defended areas, redoubts and posts were blown in and made useless for the defenders and almost every battery position was heavily shelled with gas which, when combined with the fog, became a heavy nauseating mixture. Immediately the British artillery replied to the enemy fire; where they could, they fired on their SOS lines. In their gas masks the British troops stumbled and groped their way about and made their way to their battle stations.

As the sun rose at 0600 hours the fog was still thick along the whole of the front; it was thickest on the right of Fifth Army in the valley of The Oise, the further northwards, away from the river, the thinner the fog. In other sectors the Germans were carrying out raids and barrages designed to keep the High Command guessing. In Flanders British First Army reported enemy raids and, along the French Front, the Germans fought their way into the trenches between Champagne and Navarin.

Under cover of the bombardment German engineers moved out of their trenches into No Man's Land and cut the British wire ready for the infantry assault. This was timed for 0940 hours and fell on the four Army Corps of Fifth Army north of the Oise and the VI and IV Corps of Third Army. But some German units desiring to have an early footing in the British lines attacked early; indeed, Reserve Jaeger Battalion 15 went over the top at 0614 hours. Many German units found the British Front Line manned mainly by dead men, with a few gassed and wounded desperately trying to hold on.

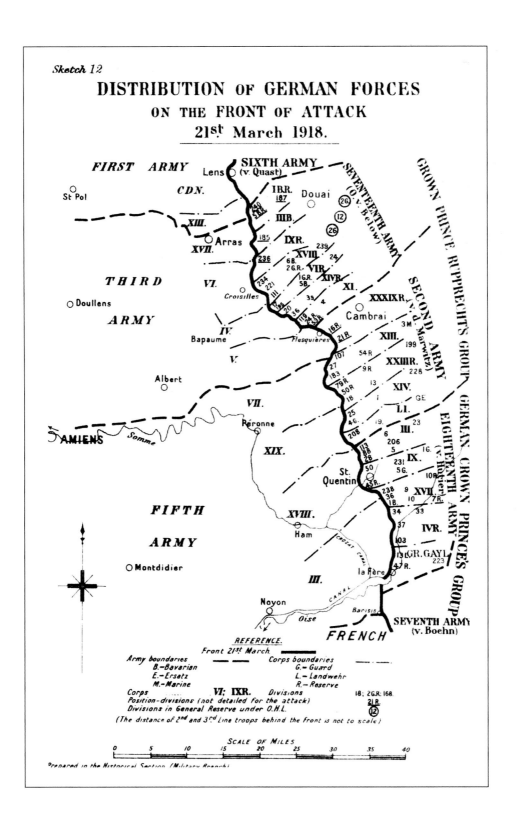

Sketch 12

DISTRIBUTION OF GERMAN FORCES
ON THE FRONT OF ATTACK
21st March 1918.

FIRST ARMY

SIXTH ARMY
Lens (v. Quast)

CDN.

St Pol

IBR.
187
Douai

IIIB.

XIII.

IXR.

Arras

XVII.

185

XVIII
68.
2G.R.
VIR
IG.R.
5B.

239
24

236

THIRD

VI.

234
221

XIVR.

XI.

Croisilles

39. 4

XXXIXR.
Cambrai

Doullans

ARMY

IV.

16R.

XIII.
3M.

Bapaume

21R.

199

Flesquières

54.R

V.

107
27
183

9.R

XXIIIR.
228

79.R
50.R
18

13

XIV.
GE

Albert

25
46.
208

19.

LI.

III.
23

VII.

Péronne

6
113
28

206
5

I.G.

AMIENS
Somme

IX.
231
5.G.

50
A.S.R.

XIX.

St.
Quentin

238
36
1.B.

9
10

XVII.
7.R.

108R

34

33

FIFTH

37

IV.R.

XVIII.

Ham

103

ARMY

13 I.G.R. GAYL.
223

Montdidier

la Fère

47.R

III.

Noyon

Oise

Barisis.

SEVENTH ARMY
(v. Boehn)

FRENCH

SEVENTEENTH ARMY
(O. v. Below)

CROWN PRINCE RUPPRECHT'S GROUP

SECOND ARMY
(v. d. Marwitz)

EIGHTEENTH ARMY
(v. Hutier)

GERMAN CROWN PRINCE'S GROUP

REFERENCE.
Front 21st March ▬▬▬▬

Army boundaries – – –
  B.–Bavarian
  E.–Ersatz
  M.–Marine

Corps boundaries — —
  G.–Guard
  L.–Landwehr
  R.–Reserve

Corps .... VI; IXR.   Divisions   18; 2G.R:168.
Position-divisions (not detailed for the attack)   21R.
Divisions in General Reserve under O.H.L.   ⑫

(The distance of 2nd and 3rd line troops behind the front is not to scale.)

SCALE OF MILES

0   5   10   15   20   25   30   35   40

Prepared in the Historical Section (Military Branch).

21

Many unexploded British heavy artillery shells, of which there appear to be a fair amount, were collected by the Germans for propaganda purposes. In the background lies the wreckage of a shot down British scout aeroplane possibly a Sopwith Pup or Camel.

A German artillery battery prepares their guns to fire the barrage that will open the March offensive in 1918.

German troops in the market place of a French village preparing for the offensive which will capture the village of Ham.

Quickly the camouflage is removed from the gun, which has been carefully hidden in the remains of a building.

A platoon of German infantry armed with a light machine gun advancing through a village on their way towards Ham. On the left lie the remains of a light railway locomotive destroyed by shell fire.

On the front line between St Quentin and Laon a severely wounded man is brought in by his comrades. They have made a makeshift stretcher out of a strip of tent canvas. (Zeltbahnen).

A handler and his specially trained dog. The animal is trained to carry first aid supplies across the open ground and find wounded men, who can then apply dressings to themselves until the stretcher bearers can find them.

A heavy machine gun mounted on a wheel in an anti-aircraft role. These units became known as FLAK, (Flug Abwehr Kanonen). The name became better known in World War II.

Behind the front line a signals unit keeps the Divisional and Corps Headquarters in touch with the men on the battlefield.

A German supply column and infantry reserves follow up the main advance down the Bapaume road.

A field howitzer battery follows up the advance over No Man's Land and across the British front line. In the foreground a British soldier lies dead. Like the British, the German photographers showed plenty of enemy dead and wounded but very few of their own.

Also following up, the advancing infantry as a pioneer storm troop – they would soon be constructing fresh artillery positions and with the Somme and the Crozat Canal to cross, their skills and equipment would prove invaluable to the men in front.

Like the British in their attacks of 1916 and 1917, the Germans hoped to be able to set the cavalry free to roll up the flanks of the enemy. Here German divisional cavalry move across the British lines. In the foreground a dead British soldier lies behind an abandoned Lewis gun which, if still operational, will soon be turned on its previous owners.

The original German caption 'die Englander bei Roupy'. The village of Roupy was in the middle of the 30th Division front and held by 2/Green Howards. Here the mist cleared by noon and the Yorkshiremen were able to repulse the German advance at 1330 hours. Later the Germans repulsed a counter-attack by one of the Green Howards companies and by 1830 hours they had broken through and gained a footing in the village. Here British dead lie in what passed for a trench during the retreat. On the left a Vickers gun lies abandoned.

In the atmosphere heavily laden with gas, a Pioneer unit follows up the leading waves of the advance.

Soon the British prisoners of war were making their way to the 'sammelplatz', the 'collecting point'; in many cases they helped or were made to help German wounded and British wounded to the Casualty Clearing Station.

'Aus dem wege zum feldlazarett durch die strassen von St Quentin.' 'On the way to the field hospital through the streets of St Quentin.' Here two British PoWs, accompanied by a German soldier, carry a wounded man to hospital in St Quentin. These men may well be from the 30th Division which held the sector in front of St Quentin.

An English PoW gives a piggy-back to a wounded German infantryman on their way back, the German to hospital, the Englishman to the PoW camp.

An unwounded British PoW has brought a severely wounded comrade to the German field dressing station and the German medical orderlies are dressing his wounds, no longer enemies but caring friends.

Here a German soldier escorts three British PoWs back to the rear, one of whom carries a wounded German infantryman on his shoulders.

Behind the front unwounded British soldiers carry their wounded comrades to the dressing station. They must have come from a good unit, for even though they are PoWs they are still marching in step. In the background German infantrymen head in the opposite direction towards the front, whilst others watch as the column goes by.

Soon the captured British soldiers were back at a makeshift cage and well behind the line. The first thing many of them did was to dump their gas masks. Just inside the gate a soldier sits on an ever-growing pile of the redundant equipment.

Here the men have started to queue for rations; it will be a long time before those at the back get a decent meal. Note nearly every man has retained his gasmask haversack to allow him to collect and carry anything he may need.

The pioneers have quickly bridged the enemy trenches and the field artillery was able to move forward in support of the infantry. Here a horse-drawn limber and gun follow up the advance.

Behind a sandbagged barricade lies a fallen Englishman. With a glass on the original, his brass shoulder title reveals him to be from the Wiltshire Regiment. Their 2nd Battalion was the only one, from the regiment, in the line on this front. At a redoubt on a low ridge called l' Epine de Dallon they fought until 1430 hours before being overwhelmed. Indeed only a handful of survivors made their way back to the British lines.

Another view of a captured trench with its garrison dead in situ. In the top left hand corner is what appears to be an unopened box of ammunition.

The leading German troops quickly overran the British rear areas and captured many ammunition dumps and stores depots. This held up the advance, for the leading infantrymen had not seen stores of such quality for many a day and they stopped to plunder the depots. Of course the propaganda of the original caption does not admit this. But here we see German soldiers searching among the captured stores.

Not only did the German Army capture large dumps of food and equipment, they also took large amounts of ammunition; this allowed them to repair captured guns and send the ammunition back to the British with a nasty effect.

A column of infantry move forward towards the line past a deep mine or shell crater.

St Quentin, March 1918: on the left a light artillery battery moves up, whilst on the right an infantry unit takes a well-earned rest. In the rear another column is forming up ready to march. On the extreme right a cavalryman, possibly employed on traffic control or working as a messenger, stands holding his horse by the bridle.

The museum in St Quentin, badly damaged by allied artillery fire: a propaganda coup for the Germans.

To keep the men at the front supplied the German Army supply columns moved forward as soon as possible. Here a supply column moves through the streets of St Quentin.

Through the devastated streets of St Quentin German infantry and artillery move up towards the front. This photograph was most likely taken prior to the beginning of the attack.

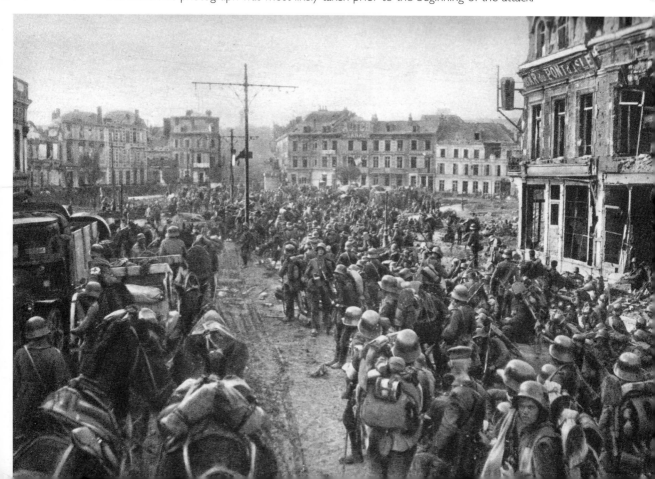

St Quentin Cathedral, badly damaged by shells; on the right a building is on fire.

The damage to the cathedral, which was hundreds of years old, was immense. Here the German photographer shows the devastation caused by British artillery.

Forward across the devastated battlefields of 1916 went the German Army. Here a reserve formation moves up into the line at Albert, which was abandoned by the British, who decided to hold higher ground to the west, on 26 March 1918.

A British artillery position near Albert; the crew have left in a hurry and not destroyed the gun.

A collecting point for wounded men. Here they receive rudimentary first aid and an anti-tetanus injection before being transported to the rear.

The remains of a British aircraft shot down in a dog fight near Albert.

In front of Albert, 'the spoils of war'; a modern artillery piece has fallen into German hands.

On the battlefield near Albert a British battery has been captured; the gun crews have pulled the guns out of the gun pits in order to engage targets over open sights.

With the ground churned up into a crater field, the German gunners struggled to get their guns forward.

A British supply column caught on an open road by the German artillery; dead orses and material are scattered all about.

Somewhere on the Somme front near Albert, the dead horses and limbers of a British artillery unit lie on the battlefield. The unused ammunition can clearly be seen in the limbers. Pieces of harness are scattered round the limber.

A British howitzer position on the northern edge of the attack near Roisel. This small town, east of Peronne, fell into British hands in the spring of 1917, but was taken again by the Germans on 22 March 1918.

After the storm at Albert, British dead lie in a hastily constructed trench. Weapons and equipment are everywhere; on the left a bandolier of ammunition lies unused, whilst further along the trench a Lewis gun points skyward.

In a sunken road near Clery, north west of Peronne, a British battery lies totally destroyed by German artillery

An infantry battalion from a second line division marches forward through the destroyed village of Hermies.

Chapter Three
The Battle continues

The success of General von Hutier's men against the British Fifth Army showed that the Germans had struck the weakest part of the British Front. The left flank of General Marwitz's Second Army had also made good progress but its right flank and General Below's Seventeenth Army had met strong resistance. After reading the reports that came in from the various armies, General Ludendorf made his plans for the following days. He decided that when the German forces had reached the line of Bapaume – Peronne – Ham, Seventeenth Army would attack towards Arras and St Pol. Second Army had the objective of Miraumont – Lihons, whilst Eighteenth Army would send strong forces via Ham in the direction of Chaulenes – Noyon. Now the Germans' main objective was to split the French and British Armies by a rapid advance on both sides of the River Somme, their aim being to drive the British into the sea and to defeat the French. Although 23 March went favourably for the Eighteenth Army and the right flank of the Second Army, by the end of the day General Below had overestimated the success of Seventeenth Army.

Although there was a gap opening between the British Third and Fifth Armies, and the Germans were thrusting into that gap, the British managed to hang on and push engineer and pioneer units, acting as infantry, into the breach. By 26 March the line had been pushed back some twenty-five miles, but the French had come up on the right and, although the German forces took Montdidier, they were eventually stopped.

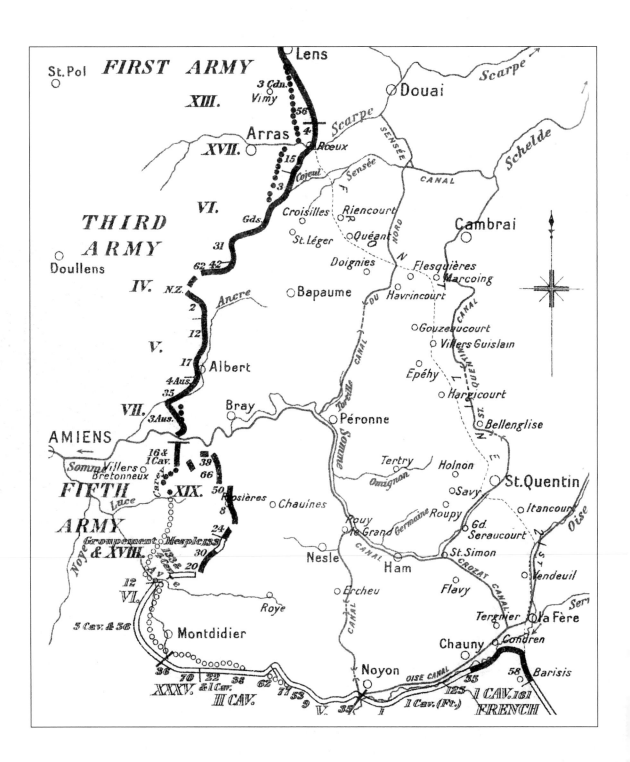

German pioneers make a dense smoke screen to hide important positions from the prying eyes of British reconnaissance aircraft.

The breech of a field gun badly damaged by artillery fire.

In the rear area near Cambrai a supply column moves toward the front

The crew of a heavily camouflaged railway gun pose for the photographer.

A heavily laden column of infantry heads towards the battle front.

A German column passes a knocked-out battery position. Unused ammunition lies beside the gun in the foreground.

British prisoners dig graves for the dead; on the left two soldiers check for identification.

Another shot of the same scene, the two British sergeants checking the pockets of the dead German soldiers. The man on the left is handing an identity disc to the German, who is making a note of the names. Some of the dead have already had their boots taken.

The heavily congested street of a destroyed French village. Infantry going back, having been relieved, pass a supply column moving up with supplies.

Gefreiter Andreas Koch served with Number 3 Company, 20 Bavarian Infantry Regiment; he fell on 4 April 1918 when his unit fought at Moreul.

Christl. Andenken im Gebete
an den tugendsamen Jüngling
Andreas Köck
Attenhuberbauerssohn von
Peterskirchen
Gefreiter beim 20. bayer. Inf.-Rgt.
3. Kompagnie
Inhaber des Eisernen Kreuzes 2. Kl.

welcher am 4. April 1918 bei einem
Sturmangriff bei Morenl im 21. Lebens-
jahre den Heldentod fürs Vaterland starb.

———

Ein junges Leben hat beendet
In schrecklich ernster Schlacht
Und bleich lag er am Rasen
Der Todesengel wacht.
Zieh ein in Himmelsfreuden,
Du tapfrer Bayernheld,
Hast gedient so treu dem König,
Nun dien' dem Herrn der Welt!

Vater unser.   Ave Maria.

Gebr. Erdl. Trostberg.

A tented camp overrun by the Germans; the stores and litter left lying about, indicates the panic that had set in among the retreating troops.

A German field artillery unit takes a break on the march. At the left rear is a field cooker and the unit baggage wagons.

On the road near Bailluel a British heavy artillery piece lies abandoned and destroyed.

An aerial photograph of Bapaume taken by German reconnaissance aircraft.

A German ammunition dump at destroyed by British aircraft.

A machine gun team wait for the order to advance.

Here an infantry section attack an enemy position; one man is just about to throw a grenade, whilst his comrades provide covering fire.

Heavy artillery on the march through Bapaume. In the background a transport column wait their turn to join the congested road.

The stumps of what was once a tree-lined road, totally destroyed by artillery fire.

A long column of British prisoners of war make their way back towards the prison camps. A large number were kept in the immediate rear area to provide labour for the Germans.

English soldiers, pushing a wounded comrade on a sack barrow, head towards the collecting point.

Another group of prisoners, among them a number of highlanders, with another wounded man on a wheelbarrow.

Men of an infantry division rest near Roupy, to the west of St Quentin.

The crew of a German 21cm mortar move it into a fire position. In the foreground shells in baskets are ready for use.

Aerial reconnaissance photograph of Peronne.

Men of Number 2 Company, Reserve Pioneer Battalion Number 82. This unit served with the 80th Reserve Division and came into the line at Sauvillers on 3 April, where the division suffered heavy losses. Marked X is Pioneer Peter Arthuis.

The totally destroyed village of Chaulnes photographed on 26 March 1918. A railway gun was brought up to the vicinity of this village and used to bombard Amiens.

A 10cm artillery battery provides support for the troops advancing towards Montdidier. The nearest gun has just fired; the barrel is in the recoiled position. Second left a gunner stands by with another shell.

A German soldier walks through the streets of Peronne towards the badly damaged cathedral.

A section of German infantrymen march past the bodies of fallen British soldiers. The dead man in the foreground wears the crossed axes of an infantry pioneer.

A machine gun team rush to take up a fire position near the crossing of the Oise.

A captured British heavy artillery position; a lot of ammunition lies ready for use, but the gunners are dead or have retreated.

Chapter Four
The Attacks in the North

On 9 April 1918 the Germans switched their attack to the north; that day, as on 21 March, a heavy mist hung over the battlefield, which did not lift until early afternoon. Shortly after 0400 hours the German batteries opened fire on the British and Portuguese, the principal targets being artillery positions, road junctions and all headquarters down to battalion level. The shelling, as on 21 March, was a mixture of high explosive and phosgene gas. Armentieres was shelled with yellow cross, mustard gas shells. The German divisions attacking against the Portuguese reported very little resistance in the front and second lines: 1st Bavarian Reserve Division said 'The trench garrisons surrendered after feeble resistance,' whilst 8th Bavarian Reserve Division reported, 'It was not until the third system was reached at 0930 hours that in places slight resistance was offered.' In the 35th Division, Infantry Regiment 141 sent back the following message, 'First system taken without resistance. In the second first prisoners taken. 0945 hours stiff resistance at strongpoint V, captured and seventy prisoners taken.'

The Germans were now hampered by the soft ground of the Valley of the Lys; artillery batteries trying to get forward stuck in the mud and the German engineers trying to construct bridges and track were hampered by British gun fire. The Germans had prepared some of their own A7V tanks for the operation but they proved too heavy for the ground; also they had ten captured British tanks back in service with iron cross markings. One broke down and blocked the route of an approaching division, upsetting the timetable.

Towards the evening of 9 April the Germans were across the Lys at Estaires. Further north Messines was captured and the attackers pushed on to Steenebeek, but here they met stout opposition and were counter-attacked on a number of occasions. Further attacks were made in the Ypres Salient against Wytshaete, whilst to the south, Armentieres was taken with the capture of 3,000 prisoners and 40 guns.

Throughout April the Germans pressed hard against the British in the north, although by the middle of the month they were attacking Mont Noir and Mont Rouge with the aim of outflanking the high ground of Mount Kemmel. But only slight gains were made on most of the line and the attack came to a standstill. On 25 April the attack was renewed and was marked by the capture of Mount Kemmel and the sector around it from the French. But eventually the attacks were brought to a standstill. The German soldier was tired and war-weary. The attacks that had started so strong and powerful ran out of steam, probably because the best of the German Army lay dead on the battlefields of France. It proved extremely difficult to replace the losses in experienced officers and NCOs.

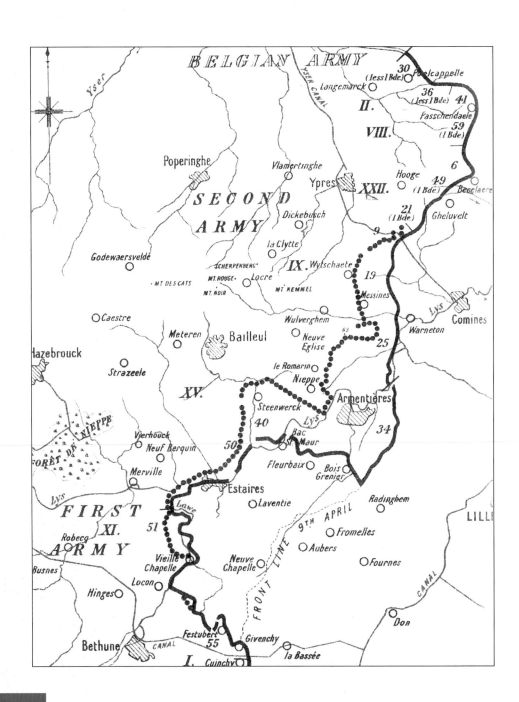

A field artillery battery on its way to a new position on the Flanders Front.

A heavy artillery piece is manhandled into position.

The guns are in position and ranging shots are fired.

Another view of the same battery in action.

The battery receives a fresh fire order and changes the angle of the guns.

A German soldier inspects the damage caused by his artillery fire. The horses and men of a
British artillery unit lie dead on the road.

The battlefield
near Arras; total
chaos, the ground
has been churned
up by the heavy
barrage.

Here a 21cm mortar battery moves its position between Bapaume and Arras in preparation for the next phase of the battle.

German infantry advance into the fog of war.

The British lines between Bapaume and Arras after they have been captured. A German soldier stands under a thick belt of barbed wire. This has been set to prevent the enemy from getting into that section of the trench; in the end, though, the trench was probably outflanked.

A sunken road near Arras; two mounted German soldiers ride past discarded material.

Pioneer Martin Thaller served with Number One Company of the 23rd Infantry Regiment, in the 12th Division. The division came into the line on the night of 23-24 March but was held up by the British artillery fire. Martin fell the following week.

English dead in Estaires; the town was held by 149 Brigade of the 50th Northumbrian Division. The Germans, led by 35th Division, forced a crossing of the Pont Levis across the River Lys and pushed the Northumberlands back.

6/Northumberland Fusiliers was mostly made up of young lads fresh out from England. However they put up a magnificent defence and fought hard to retake the town, getting to within one hundred yards of the bridge. Here two British soldiers, most likely from that battalion, lie in the ruins of the houses they fought to retake.

Advancing just south of Estaires was the 8th Bavarian Reserve Division. They lost 50% of their effective strength between 9 and 14 April. Among those to fall was Soldat Martin Birner, who served with Number 6 Company, 19th Bavarian Reserve Regiment.

The Germans used quite a lot of gas during the offensive and after they captured Armentieres they had to put up warning signs to keep their own troops safe: 'Yellow Cross Gas' 'Don't drink the water,' 'Don't enter the houses.'

The front line near Armentieres, the sector held by the Portuguese, where the Germans launched the attack.

Another view of the trenches in this sector. The bombardment has destroyed the position.

German troops force their way past a barricade to enter Bailluel.

In the war-damaged streets of Bailleul a German patrol moves cautiously forward, checking that the defenders have left.

The market place in Bailleul; a British shell explodes as the photographer takes his shot.

The main door of the cathedral in Bauilleul: the devastation caused by an artillery barrage

The hotel de ville
and the church in
Bailleul market
place.

French and British prisoners of war march towards the rear, passing on the right a German Casualty Clearing Station. Note the Red Cross flag.

The bombed-out streets of Armentieres. The town fell to the 6th Army on 11 April.

An artillery barrage bursts on the heights of Notre Dame de Lorette or, as the German infantrymen knew it, Hill 165, the Lorettehohe.

Some German marine artillery units were mounted in barges and brought up along the French canal network to provide support fire for the attacking infantry.

Having been relieved, these three German machine gunners pose for the photographer on 22 April 1918. Note the machine gunner arm badge on the seated man and his friend on the right. The original card is marked, in German, 'In the field 22 April 1918 a memento of your friend Ludwig Bortenach.'

The advancing Germans did not have everything their own way. Here a field ambulance unit has come under British artillery fire and suffered casualties.

A typical German battlefield photograph; British dead lie on the edge of their trench.

A severely damaged British howitzer battery put out of action by the German artillery.

British prisoners carry a wounded comrade to the German dressing station.

An infantry section fights its way through a partially destroyed French village.

A German infantry unit moves forward into the line in artillery formation.

A heavy artillery piece provides support fire for the infantry.

In preparation for the attacks in Flanders, reconnaissance aircraft were busy taking photographs of the British lines. Here the pilot has taken a picture of the ruins of Passchendaele village.

The crater fields of Flanders; many men of both sides would simply drown and disappear after slipping into the water-filled shell holes.

Zonnebeke Lake; this ground had been fought over since October 1914. Taken by the British in 1917, it was retaken by the German 4th Army in April 1918.

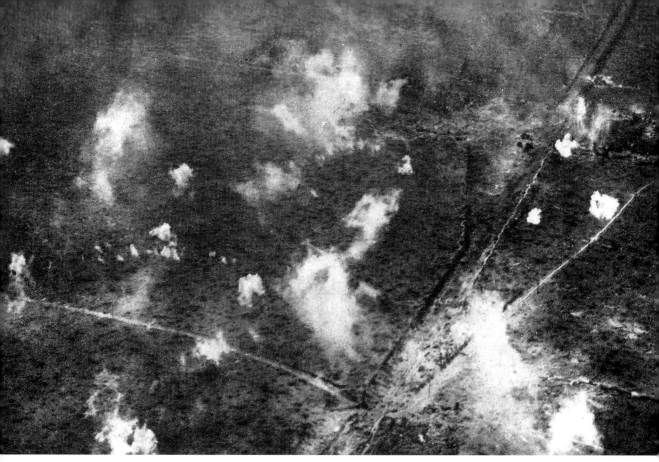

The white puffs of smoke are from British anti-aircraft shells bursting below the German reconnaissance aircraft, which is busy reporting the results, and correcting the fall of the shots of the German barrage.

A view of reserve trenches on the edge of the crater fields.

A German heavy artillery unit on the open battlefield near Hollebeke, south-east of Ypres.

Officer cadets of Infantry Regiment 162 prior to the opening of the April offensive. This regiment served with 17th Reserve Division which in 1917 had suffered heavily. Selected non-commissioned officers were sent to the 9th Reserve Corps, Officer Cadet School, and promoted to replace losses in officers.

In the desolate landscape of the Ypres Salient, a German supply wagon moves down a plank road near Hollebeke.

German soldiers move across the swamps near Gheluvelt, south-east of Ypres.

Troops of a German 'Eisenbahnbaukompagnie', roughly translated, a railway construction company, are employed repairing a road in order to get stores and munitions up to the front.

An aerial photograph of a plank road constructed across the craters and swamps of the salient.

A German observation balloon and its winding wagon have been manhandled into the area just behind the front line. From the balloon, artillery observation officers will be able to direct the fire of the various field and heavy artillery units, onto targets in the British lines.

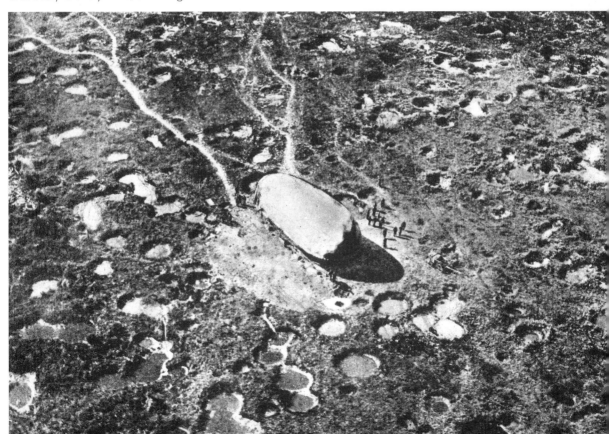

The winch gear and associated equipment is dragged and pulled through the morass.

Another reconnaissance photograph of a British-held village in the salient. On the right-hand edge of the village the trench system with its traverses and fire bays can be clearly seen.

To protect their balloons the German Army developed the 8.8cm gun mounted on the back of a lorry, 'Kraftwagonflakgeshutz'. These FLAK, 'flugabwehrkanonen,' units were able to move quickly about the rear area and especially at Cambrai were used in an anti-tank role; the forerunner of the much feared 88 of the second war.

Near Kemmel, a ground mounted anti-aircraft gun waits for Britsh aircraft to appear overhead.

Two German soldiers walk along the road past a signpost for Kemmel.

The crater-riddled slopes of Mount Kemmel.

A German soldier crosses a ditch on the battlefield at Kemmel; here the British machine guns cut down the advancing waves of German infantry. Some units tried to press home their attack but were repeatedly cut down, suffering heavy casualties. Despite the German anti-aircraft guns the Royal Air Force carried out many bombing and strafing missions over the German lines.

The crew of a heavy gun, with the assistance of some infantrymen, manhandle it into a fire position on the battlefield at Kemmel.

A German howitzer battery at the opening of the barrage on Mount Kemmel. The guns have been brought forward across the crater fields to provide close support to the infantry.

Here a field howitzer has just fired and the crew are getting ready to reload.

Men of an infantry signal section busy laying a field telephone cable. The man second on the left has a drum of cable on his back.

Infantrymen in a reserve position at Mount Kemmel; they would soon come under a very heavy British barrage.

A munitions column moves forward with stores for the front line during the Kemmel battles.

A mixture of British and French prisoners of war transport wounded German soldiers in hand carts towards the dressing stations in the rear area.

British dead lie along a road strewn with weapons and equipment. Some of the dead have had their boots taken.

Chapter Five

The Attacks on the Chemin des Dames, the Aisne and the Marne

In May 1918 General Foch had suggested an exchange of tired British divisions in exchange for fresh French divisions. Sir Douglas Haig, after checking with London, agreed, but only to sending five divisions instead of the ten to fifteen divisions suggested. It was arranged that four of the divisions selected should be sent to the French Sixth Army on the Aisne and one division would go to the French Fourth Army near Chalons sur Marne. The divisions selected, 8th (Regular), 21st (New Army), 25th (New Army) and 50th (Northumbrian) would go to the Aisne and 19th (Western) Division was stationed in the area of St Germain la Ville about seven miles from Chalons sur Marne. To command the divisions, IX Corps Headquarters, under the command of Lieutenant General A H Gordon, moved to the new area at the end of April. All these divisions had suffered heavily in the German attacks in March and April and were in desperate need of time, to come up to strength and train such reinforcements that had arrived.

The British General Staff was not happy about the choice of the Aisne Front, for they knew that it was one of the sectors that the Germans had selected for an attack. However the French assured them that the front was suitable and that things were quiet on that front.

The troops arrived and were pleased with the front which, apart from a few raids, was quite quiet; the landscape was beautiful compared to the crater-strewn landscape of Flanders. But late in April the troops began to notice suspicious movement behind the German lines. There was great activity at night, sounds of marching troops and the rumble of wagons, and in No Man's Land working parties could be heard whispering to each other. On 22 May reconnaissance aircraft of the Royal Flying Corps reported dust clouds on the roads leading to the Chemin des Dames and in the evening of the following two days more dust clouds were reported. Then two prisoners taken by the French XI Corps confirmed that an attack was imminent.

At 0100 hours on 27 May the barrage was opened all along a thirty-eight kilometre front from Berr au Bac to Chavignon. Over 1,000 artillery batteries took part in the firing. The tactics of the barrage were changed so that in the first ten minutes every gun and trench mortar fired gas shells at the highest rate of fire, at every target possible, spreading as far back as the British divisional headquarters. After this ten minute barrage the batteries changed to a mixture of high explosive and gas, whilst the trench mortars concentrated on the destruction of the British forward defences. The preparations of the barrage had been so thorough that the German infantry just had to go over and take possession of the front line, where most of the defenders were dead or quickly captured.

It was on the front of the French 22nd Division that the main blow struck; here five German divisions went over the top and by 0530 hours they had taken that part of the Chemin des Dames that fell into their sector. In some sectors bridges over the Aisne fell to the Germans intact, but on the front of 8th and 50th Divisions the British were able to destroy many of the crossings over the river and the canal, and at Pontavert the bridge was destroyed on the initiative of a French non-commissioned officer.

Although the attack had gone well for the Germans they didn't have it all their own way and Seventh Army ordered the leading troops not to allow the pursuit to slacken during the night. One of the problems encountered was that as the advancing men came across dumps of stores and alcohol, they stopped advancing and got drunk. On the flanks little headway was made but in the centre a great bulge was pushed into the French and British line. The great dumps of food that were captured solved one problem for the German high command. It allowed the transport to concentrate on the carriage of ammunition. By the beginning of June the fighting had almost died out. The German attack had once again been well planned and executed but again they had the problem of holding a large bulge in the enemy line with tired troops, with questionable morale.

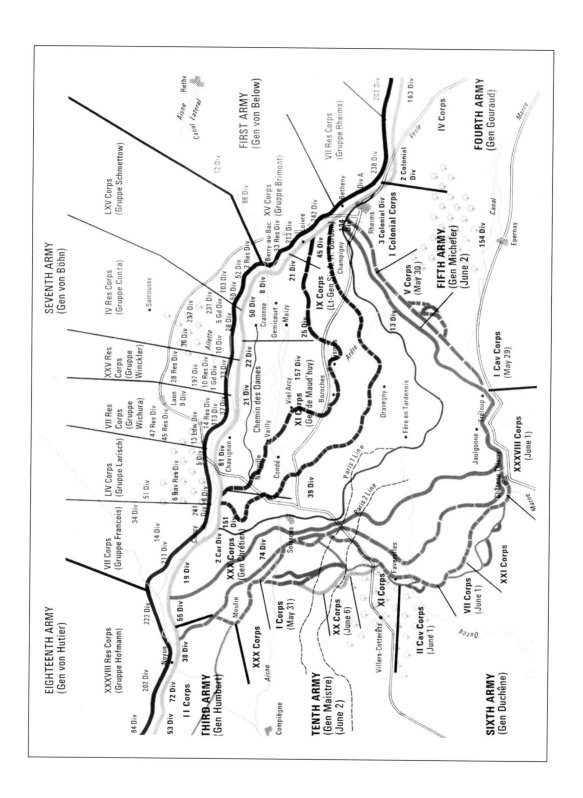

EIGHTEENTH ARMY
(Gen von Hutier)

SEVENTH ARMY
(Gen von Böhn)

FIRST ARMY
(Gen von Below)

FOURTH ARMY
(Gen Gouraud)

XXXVIII Res Corps
(Gruppe Hofmann)

VII Corps
(Gruppe Francois)

LIV Corps
(Gruppe Larisch)

VII Res Corps
(Gruppe Wichura)

XXV Res Corps
(Gruppe Winckler)

IV Res Corps
(Gruppe Conta)

LXV Corps
(Gruppe Schmettow)

XV Corps (Gruppe Brimont)

VII Res Corps
(Gruppe Rheims)

84 Div

202 Div

72 Div

53 Div

II Corps

Noyon

223 Div

38 Div

55 Div

14 Div

211 Div

34 Div

51 Div

6 Bav Res Div

5 Div

241

19 Div

Compiègne

Aisne

THIRD ARMY
(Gen Humbert)

XXX Corps

Coucy

61 Div

Chavignon

16 Div

2 Car Div

151 Div

XXX Corps
(Gen Chrétien)

74 Div

Soissons

Moulin

I Corps
(May 31)

47 Res Div

45 Res Div

13 Erfw Div

113 Div

14 Res Div

27 Div

Neuville

Condé

39 Div

Vailly

21 Div

22 Div

Chemin des Dames

10 Res Div

9 Div

Laon

1 Gd Div

28 Res Div

197 Div

33 Div

36 Div

231 Div

10 Div

Ailette

Gemicourt

Maizy

Craonne

50 Div

8 Div

Berry-au-Bac

7 Res Div

52 Div

103 Div

60 Div

28 Div

5 Gd Div

Samoussy

86 Div

12 Div

Aisne
Canal Lateral

Rethe

Viel Arcy

157 Div

XI Corps
(Gen de Maud'huy)

Bazoches

Aisne

Ardre

Vesle

213 Div

33 Res Div

Loivre

45 Div

25 Div

21 Div

IX Corps
(Lt-Gen Sir A. Gordon)

13 Div

Champigny

134 Div

Rheims

242 Div

3 Colonial Div

V Corps
(May 30)

Betheny

Div A

238 Div

2 Colonial
Div

3 Colonial Corps

I Colonial Corps

FIFTH ARMY
(Gen Micheler)
(June 2)

154 Div

Epernay

IV Corps

163 Div

203 Div

Marne

Canal

TENTH ARMY
(Gen Maistre)
(June 2)

I Corps
(May 31)

XX Corps
(June 6)

Villers-Cotterêts

XI Corps

Faverolles

Ourcq

II Cav Corps
(June 1)

Paris 1 Line

Paris 2 Line

Dravegny

Fère en Tardenois

Marne

Château Thierry

Jaulgonne

XXXVIII Corps
(June 1)

Tréloup

I Cav Corps
(May 29)

VII Corps
(June 1)

XXI Corps

SIXTH ARMY
(Gen Duchêne)

95

A field battery prepares to fire a barrage.

A howitzer
battery waits in
the shelter of a
sunken road for
the order to
advance.

German soldiers move along a sunken road near La Ville aux Bois.

The woods beyond La Ville aux Bois destroyed by German artillery fire.

In the woods
beyond La Ville
aux Bois
German soldiers
inspect the ruins
of a British field
dressing station.

A heavy mortar battery in position and waiting for fire orders.

Field guns are hooked on to their limber by sweating gunners as the order to move has been received.

Men of a balloon unit prepare the balloon for hoisting. The artillery observation officers will soon be directing the fire of many guns onto British or French positions. The iron cross markings stand out on the top and side of the balloon's fabric.

Artillery observers in a position near Berry au Bac watch the barrage fall on the British trenches.

The view of the Aisne from Hill 108 at Berry Au Bac; the forward trenches can be clearly seen from above.

Men of a machine gun unit carry their weapons and ammunition forward to the Chemin de Dames or, as it was known to the German soldier, 'Der Damenweg'.

An infantry section in the open, away from the trenches, ready to advance.

Here heavily laden men of an assault engineer unit move explosives into the battle area by hand cart.

Behind the front a dog handler has brought his wounded dog to the 'Hund Lazarett', the dog hospital, for treatment. The Germans used trained dogs to carry messages and look for wounded men with a small first aid kit strapped to the dog's back.

In the fight for the British trenches at Berry au Bac, a minenwerfer unit moves forward through a gap in the barbed wire.

A typical scene on the Chemin des Dames, the trees have been destroyed and the land ploughed up by the artillery barrage.

Waiting in readiness to move, men of an artillery unit relax before advancing towards the Chemin des Dames.

On 27 May 1918 German infantry assaulted the British and French positions along the Aisne. The first wave, having taken the position, are resting as a follow-up unit passes through them to continue the assault.

'Vormarsch schnell', 'Advance quickly'; German Infantry move forward at the double, towards the Aisne crossings.

Where the bridges were destroyed the German engineers were very quick to erect foot bridges, to prevent the advance slowing down.

During the fighting on the Chemin des Dames, on the German right, an infantry column heads towards the high ground between Pargny and Chavignon above the Aisne Canal.

This bridge across the Aisne was blown up, but its destruction wasn't complete and although artillery couldn't get across the infantry could and thereby continued the advance.

Having stormed the river crossings at Pont Arcy on the Aisne, the front line infantry rush forward across a road under machine gun fire.

A French 75mm gun lies abandoned in its position on the Chemin des Dames.

As the German troops advanced they came across abandoned stores and dumps. Here they have taken a train with a truck loaded with casks of wine. In the foreground on the left a soldier enjoys a drink, to the right two men are filling their water bottles. Others are busy getting the barrels off the truck.

A German supply column moves along the road towards a burning village; on the left on the edge of the field an infantry unit rests.

As on the other fronts, long lines of prisoners of war started to make their way towards the rear.

French prisoners have been made to assist German pioneers repair the road in order that supply wagons can move up to the line.

A divisional supply column formed up ready to move off and follow the advancing infantry.

German transport, both horse-drawn and lorries, in the market place of a French village.

Here a column of French prisoners of war carrying their wounded are escorted to the rear; on the right German soldiers watch as they pass by.

This Frenchman with a wounded foot is given a ride in a wheelbarrow by his friend.

A column of French prisoners are escorted away from the battle area.

At Berry au Bac British prisoners carry a wounded German over the Aisne Canal on a wooden foot bridge erected by German pioneers.

A wounded Frenchman is carried shoulder high into captivity, by four of his comrades.

French artillerymen and horses lie dead near a hutted camp, the target of the German artillery.

On the battlefield between the Aisne and the Marne, the British and French left so quickly that they could only destroy their stores dumps. Here German soldiers try to salvage un-burnt provisions.

The destroyed village of Chavignon, just south of the Aisne Canal. German troops stormed through this village on their way to the heights of the Chemin des Dames in May 1918.

This stores dump was totally destroyed before it could fall into German hands.

From the air a reconnaissance pilot took this photograph of a burning dump with the smoke from the fire rising high into the sky.

The infantry move forward in readiness to storm the crossing on the Aisne Canal.

In the communication zone behind the battle area an ammunition column has been destroyed at a railway crossing.

A burning dump; stores and tins of food burn after being set on fire by their former owners before they left.

Four British 'Tommies' pull a severely wounded comrade on a hand cart.

The blood-soaked battlefield of the Winterburg, the highest point on the Chemin des Dames.

Infantry move across a bridge over the Aisne Canal that has been taken intact; this greatly assisted the forward movement of the German troops.

This artillery ammunition dump, with overhead cover for the shells, was taken before the retreating troops could set fire to it.

A severely wounded German soldier is carried on a stretcher to the field dressing station; after delivering the wounded man the prisoners will be taken to the collecting point, in order to be taken further back.

On the Chemin des Dames, worn out British prisoners rest on the side of the road watching a heavily laden German supply column move forward.

This French 164mm gun was captured in its fire position two kilometres south-west of Pargny.

A dead British soldier lies on the battlefield near Cormicy. The British 21st Division was holding the front line here and was attacked by the German 33rd Reserve Division.

German infantry in their frontline trench waiting for the order to advance.

An artillery battery moves into position on the Chemin des Dames.

Fire orders have been received and a shell is on its way towards the French or British defenders.`

In the newly captured town of Cormicy a German field ambulance unit sets up its dressing station in the ruins of the destroyed church.

Two German soldiers survey the landscape after the breakthrough on the Winterberg, the highest point of the Chemin des Dames.

In this photograph, taken in May or June 1918 on the Marne, a German battery is out in the open firing towards Givecourt. By the time they were brought to a halt the Germans were only 85 kilometres from Paris.

This French defensive position, in front of Soissons, stands empty after the hurried departure of its garrison.

A German soldier stands looking at the damage caused to a village by an artillery barrage. The church has been destroyed so that its tower could not be used as an observation post.

This gun has been manhandled out on to the road and is firing over open sights at a target down the road.

A mixed group of British and French prisoners taken during the Battle of The Aisne, waiting with German wounded to be taken to the rear.

Having been taken by German troops the village of Vincelles is now being shelled by French artillery.

The ruins of Soissons.

The Rue St Martin in Soissons; the street was destroyed by French artillery trying to drive the Germans out.

Looking towards the cathedral past the burning ruins of Soissons.

In the front line near Soissons two medical orderlies treat a wounded man.

A casualty of the air war over Soissons, the pilot of a fighter plane lies dead beside the wreckage of his machine.

Between the Aisne and the Marne, a storm battalion moves forward to engage the enemy.

The same view later in the day, French prisoners walk unescorted towards the German rear positions.

Wounded, both German and British, at an aid post in the line. Note the large diamond battle patch worn on the shoulder of the British soldier on the right. He is possibly from 151 Brigade, the Durham Light Infantry Brigade serving with 50th (Northumbrian) Division.

An ammunition column on the move, passing the badly damaged church in the French town of Cormicy.

Chapter Six
Other French Fronts

Throughout June and July the German Army continued to press the French and British in various sectors. In Flanders and on the Somme south of Montdidier, as well as the Marne, various attacks took place and now withdrawals were taking place. The Imperial German Army was not what it had been; casualties and low morale were taking effect. The German 'Feldgrau' or 'Landser' was showing signs of war-weariness and when they learned that American troops were now on the Western Front many German soldiers believed they could no longer win.

The breech of the railway gun in the next photograph.

This huge French railway gun was taken intact by the Germans.

A large number of French prisoners taken in Champagne.

French artillery shells land on the German-held positions near Craonne, south-east of Laon, near the slopes of the Chemin des Dames.

Supposedly a photograph of the French troops in their front line. However it is obviously a posed photograph for people back in Germany. No front line soldier would have stood with his head above the parapet like that. Nor would a photographer stand up to take such a picture.

Aerial photograph of fort Douamont at Verdun. By flying reconnaissance missions over this sector of the front and making the French think they would attack here, the Germans kept much needed reinforcements away from the other fronts where they were attacking.

The cathedral stands high among the ruins of the town of Rethel.

German infantry in the forest near Leiz. The forest has been destroyed by the artillery barrage.

The remains of the French fort 'Camp des Romains', near St Mihiel.

The Argonne front was relatively quiet compared to other areas and the troops were able to construct well-made accommodation for themselves; however throughout the period of the 1918 offensives the Germans kept making threats of an attack in order to pin down French troops on that front.

A well-made and camouflaged French bunker, with German soldiers on the top.

A huge cave near Chavignon; there was room inside to house a whole battalion.

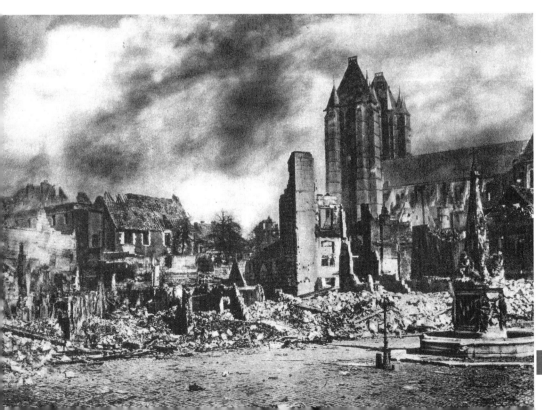

The historic cathedral of Noyon stands amid the burning ruins of the town.

German Infantry moving towards the Marne. This aerial photograph taken by a German reconnaissance pilot clearly shows the huge craters on the left and right of the road.

In Champagne a German storm battalion rushes towards the French lines.

Chriſtliches Andenken im Gebete
an den ehrengeachteten Jüngling
Jakob Alberer
Gradl-Bauersſohn von Kaſtl
Unteroffizier beim bayr. 2. Inf.-Rgt.
Inhaber des Eiſernen Kreuzes II. Klaſſe
und des Militär-Verdienſtkreuzes III. Klaſſe
welcher am 24. März 1918 nach faſt
vierjähriger treuer Felddienſtleiſtung
durch eine ſchwere Verwundung an der
Weſtfront im Alter von 26 Jahren den
Heldentod fürs Vaterland geſtorben iſt.

Liebe Eltern und Geſchwiſter gedenket mein
Ich kehr zu Euch ja nicht mehr heim.
Meine letzte Stimme, mein letzter Blick
Schickte noch Grüße an Euch zurück.
Und als ich ſtarb im Feindesland
Reichte mir keines von Euch mehr die Hand.
Gute Eltern und Geſchwiſter nicht mehr komm'
ſich zurück
Beweint mich nicht — beneidet mir mein Glück.

Mein Jeſus Barmherzigkeit!
Süßes Herz Jeſu, ſei meine Liebe!
Süßes Herz Mariä, ſei meine
Rettung!

Druck von Gebr Geiſelberger, Altötting.

Unteroffizier Jakob Alberer served with 2 Bavarian Infantry Regiment; he died on 24 March 1918 after being severely wounded.

In the fortress of Laon a large number of French prisoners are held prior to being moved to camps in Germany.

A French battery position on the Marne after being overrun by the advancing German infantry.

A German soldier rides along a road near the high ground at La Ville aux Bois.

Although the French managed to destroy the main bridge, German pioneers and engineers soon had a well-constructed wooden bridge over the Aisne at Pontavert, north-west of Reims.

French and German wounded are treated in a field hospital set up in the chateau at Pinon.

German troops and French prisoners have repaired the track so that ammunition wagons can get forward during the advance on the Marne.

A large 24cm gun captured during the advance towards the Marne in 1918.

A heavy machine gun on an anti-aircraft mounting is used against enemy aircraft. Possibly a posed photograph with the aircraft drawn onto the picture.

A field artillery battery seen making its way towards the front during the advance in May 1918.

The battery has turned off the road between Craonelle and Baslieux and into a field ready to take up a fire position.

A German column makes its way through a French village. The lorries appear to be trying to get past the men on foot.

Soldiers of Grenadier Regiment Number 10, serving with 11th Infantry Division. They came into action against the French at Montdiier where the division suffered heavily and failed to take its objective.

Taken during the advance towards the Marne in 1918. Infantry reserves pass through the destroyed village of Craonelle.

Overrun in its fire position, a large French artillery piece taken intact by the Germans on the battlefield near Reims.

These French colonial troops from Senegal lie dead on the battlefield near Reims.

An artillery limber lies on Hill 186 near Reims, the horses and gunners killed by shrapnel from the German guns. One of the gunners can be seen under the limber.

In the distance across the plain, the cathedral and town of Reims comes under German shellfire; already the town is burning. This photograph was taken by an artillery observer up in a balloon.

Two German soldiers survey the smoking ruins of Soissons after the town has fallen to the German Army in May 1918.

This French soldier fell in the bitter hand-to-hand struggle in the street, fighting for Soissons.

In this photograph a large number of French prisoners of war are collected together in the woods near Reims.

Men of a German reserve division make their way across the battlefield towards Reims.

On the battlefield between the Aisne and the Marne lies the destroyed fort at Conde, eight kilometres east of Soissons.

German Cavalry on the march. With the advent of the tank and machine gun the days of the cavalry were numbered.

Near the village of Mareuil a French 21cm lies silent, its barrel pointing skyward. On the left is the crane used for hoisting the heavy ammunition into the barrel.

In the woods near Tracy le Val a machine gun section takes a rest before continuing to advance.

German infantry leave their trenches to advance near Montdidier in June 1918.

Near Montdidier a huge gun has been destroyed.

A French Hotchkisss machine gun lies abandoned on the high ground south east of Mareuil.

A French soldier lies dead in a hurriedly constructed trench on the high ground near Mareuil.

During the Battle of the Aisne a large group of French prisoners are escorted to the rear.

The crew of a 'minenwerfer' jump up to reload having just fired the weapon.

A bridge over the Somme – Scheldte Canal, destroyed by French engineers to hold up the German advance.

Chapter Seven
Tanks

When the tank was first used against the Germans it caused panic amongst the German infantrymen who came up against the new weapon. Once they had defeated the machine, the Germans were anxious to show the German public that the 'wonder weapon' could be defeated and took a number of propaganda photographs of knocked-out machines. They even resorted to moving machines about and taking photographs from different angles to make it look as though they had knocked out more machines than they had.

They are included here to complement the photographs used in Chapter One.

F13 nose down in a ditch.

Another view of F13; it has been moved but the markings give it away.

Yet another picture of the same tank; this time it has been turned round and is facing into the field but again the 3 of Hearts on the side identifies the tank. Also the un-ditching beam is in the same angle in all three photographs. Close inspection reveals the face of the German soldier in the driving seat.

Trying to cross the bridge was the undoing of this tank; it was too heavy for the bridge which has collapsed under the weight.

The remains of a tank totally destroyed by gunfire.

Two tanks, a male with 6 pounder guns and the female, F 30, armed with machine guns, lie knocked out in a French field.

In this photograph a female tank lies tail down in a ditch. On the right hand side a door lies open after the crew have escaped.

A later view of C51; compare this to the photograph of the same machine in Chapter One.

Another view of F13. Careful inspection shows the 3 of Hearts on the side and the angle of the un-ditching beam gives it away.

A German reconnaissance aircraft took this photograph of British infantry sheltering beside a tank in the snow. The white dots are the helmets and faces of the men as they look up towards the enemy aircraft.

In the soft mud of the Ypres Salient this tank has bogged down and is gradually disappearing.

During the retreats of March and April 1918, many tanks had to be abandoned; their crews removed the Lewis guns and fought on as infantry. Here three tanks lie where their crews left them.

A flamethrower is used to fight the tank that can be seen just above the smoke.

A tank moves through the German barrage, most likely taken on a training area behind the lines after the tank was captured.

A carefully posed photograph of the same tank, supposedly on fire after being hit; probably achieved by the use of smoke grenades.

By April 1918 the Germans had their own tank, the A7V in service. At Villers Bretonneux on 24 April, thirteen A7Vs were sent into action; the British infantry panicked and ran away exactly the same as the German infantry had when faced by the British tanks. It was here that the first tank-versus-tank battle took place, when a male Mark V, of A Company of 1st Battalion Tank Corps, met 'Elfriede'. The German tank ran up a bank and rolled over onto its side. Of the two A7V with it, one was abandoned by its crew and the other retreated before it could be engaged.

A flamethrower crew demonstrate the effect use of their weapon against the tank.